Finding

STRENGTH FOR
THE JOURNEY

BIBLE STUDY GUIDE

with quotes from

Five Loaves and Two Bowls of Borscht

by **Janice Lemke**

Purpose Press
www.purposepress.net
info@purposepress.net

ISBN 978-0-9845949-1-7

Printed in the United States of America

Finding STRENGTH FOR THE JOURNEY

Introduction:
God calls Christians to different types of ministry—it might be in
Mongolia or Milwaukee, to teens in trouble or toddlers at home.
Sometimes we feel fulfilled, sometimes we don't. If we don't feel
satisfied, is it time to move on? This Bible study series explores the theme
of perseverance but touches on other topics: discovering God's will,
relationships, contentment, and benefit from trials. It gives tips on how to
handle depression, stress, and conflict.

Finding Strength for the Journey includes thirty Bible studies. It can be
used for individual study or group discussion. Each lesson includes a quote
from the book, *Five Loaves and Two Bowls of Borscht,* questions for
consideration, scriptures to read, and a space to write a "prayer of
application." Use this space to bring before God elements of the study you
want developed in your life. If used for group discussion, each lesson
begins with a "connection question" to help participants get to know each
other. In the back, you will find tips for leaders, followed by blank pages
for extra notes or prayer requests.

Five Loaves and Two Bowls of Borscht is an account of how one couple
found strength from God for ministry in Ukraine. Some quotes taken from
the book have been altered to provide context for those who don't have a
copy. It is not necessary to have this book in order to use the study. Those
wanting to read the rest of the story can order a copy from the website
www.purposepress.net or enquire at info@purposepress.net.

May God bless you and give you strength for the journey!

Janice Lemke

TABLE OF CONTENTS

1- STRENGTHEN YOUR SERVE

QUOTE from the Prologue

Galatians 6:9: "Let us not become weary in doing good, for at the proper time we will reap a harvest if we do not give up."

"How did you like it over there?" I heard this question often after my husband and I spent four years in Ukraine with our two little girls.

I battled with cockroaches in my kitchen and carried heavy groceries from the local outdoor market. The entrance to our apartment building smelled like stale urine or worse. We had no hot water—and often, no water or electricity at all. I thought mission life is supposed to be exciting and fulfilling. Picking dead bugs from rolled oats isn't my idea of fun. It's depressing to live among people in despair.

"Life in Ukraine was more difficult than expected," I replied, "but in the end, we saw more results than we anticipated." (p.7)

CONNECT: (for group study and discussion)
What's your name and where did you grow up?

STUDY AND DISCUSS:

Who is an example of perseverance to you? What inspires you about this person?

Read the following verses. Note who had what ministry.
Acts 9:36,39

Acts 16:14-15

1 Cor 9:16-18

Phil 2:25

Col. 4:12

Service to God can take many different forms, but we all have something to offer. Our ministry may be in a public arena or in a quiet corner. In what capacity is God calling you to serve Him?

How do the following verses help us set priorities for our lives? Note key phrases.
2 Cor. 5:9

2 Cor. 5:14-15

Rom. 14:7-8

Col. 3:23

Write Gal. 6:9 in your own words.

What circumstances cause you to "become weary" or tempt you to give up?

Galatians 6:9 promises, "we will reap a harvest if we do not give up." What can help you persevere?

Read the following scriptures and write down reasons to persevere:
2 Chron. 15:7

1 Cor. 15:58

Heb. 6:10-11

What concepts in Heb. 12:1-3 help you persevere?

PRAYER OF APPLICATION:

2 - TRUSTING GOD WITH THE UNKNOWN

QUOTE from Chapter 1 — "Are We There Yet?"

The place wasn't much, but I decided it would do, at least for a while. It was far from the market, far from any store. There was no phone, no running water and no refrigerator—but we wouldn't be there long. I'd been camping before. They would find us an apartment soon, or so we understood.

Cory and I put our thin lumpy mattresses on the floor in the girls' room so we could be near them in this strange new place. Mosquitoes sang but we soon fell asleep, exhausted.

I awoke around 3:30 a.m. and couldn't sleep again. The lumps in my mattress seemed more pronounced. Varmints above the ceiling scratched and scampered back and forth. I lay in the darkness and waited for morning. What had we gotten ourselves into?

I felt a bit like Abraham. I could identify with the description of him in Hebrews, "He went out, not knowing where he was going." He probably wondered how it would all turn out. He had seen God's faithfulness before, though, and I had too. (p.11-12)

CONNECT or REFLECT:
Where did you stay, in your earliest memory of spending the night away from home?

STUDY AND DISCUSS:
What was a time you found it difficult to trust God with the unknown?

What helps you trust God with the unknown?

Read about people of faith in Heb. 11. List five people and note how they trusted God with the unknown. What do you learn about faith from them?

Some say that if you have enough faith, things will go well. What might those mentioned in Heb.11:35-38 tell us about faith?

Abraham went out, not knowing where he was going (v. 8-10). Could you do that?

Why do you think he could?

What phrase from 1 Sam. 7:12 can help us face the uncertainties of the future?

What do the following scriptures show about God's character?
Jer. 29:11

Is. 40:10-11

Ps. 46:1-3

Rom 8:38-39

Phil. 4:19

Rom. 11:33-36

Prov.3:5-6

What qualities of God's character help you trust Him with the unknown?

List ways you have seen God's faithfulness.

Is God calling you to step out in some area, trusting Him with the unknown? If so, how?

PRAYER OF APPLICATION:

3 - PERSONALITY DIFFERENCES: HELP OR HINDRANCE?

QUOTE from Chapter 2 — "I Didn't Come Here for Adventure"

I'd finally had a good night's sleep so I felt ready to explore. "Do you want to go for a walk?" I asked Cory.

"No, I'll stay here," he replied. "I didn't come to Ukraine looking for adventure."

"Ok, but I've got to get out. Come on girls, let's go for a walk." I took Janelle and Alicia by the hand.

"Be careful," Cory called as I stepped outside.

Instead of taking the longer road, we headed straight down the hill, walking on a rocky path. I felt disappointed Cory didn't join us on this outing, but I accepted our differences. He's a "look-before-you-leap" kind of guy. I just jump in and figure out later what I got myself into. He worried about our safety, but I wondered how he would adapt in a country where so much lay out of his control.

I had asked him once, "Why can't you be more spontaneous?" He replied, "I don't know, I'm just not that way." Fortunately, he never asked me, "Why aren't you more organized?" We had our own strengths and worked well together as a team. (p.18)

CONNECT or REFLECT:

How are you different from your siblings or others in your family?

STUDY AND DISCUSS:

How would you describe someone who has a low tolerance for differences in others?

(Consider: Do any of those characteristics fit you?)

Personality differences in people close to us can cause conflict. How *should* we respond to such differences?

What helps us accept those differences instead of being irritated by them?

How do the following verses answer that question?
Rom. 12:10,16

Rom. 15:7

1 Cor. 13:1-7

Col. 3:12-15

In light of the verses above, when considering someone who irritates you, what can you do differently?

God created personality differences and differing spiritual gifts. How can they make us stronger as a team?

How do the following scriptures affirm the importance of differences?
1 Cor. 12:4-31

Rom. 12:4-8

Differing abilities or gifts can contribute to feelings of superiority or inferiority. How can we avoid either tendency?

What advice do the following scriptures give?
Rom 12:3

Rom 12:16

Rom 9:20-21

1 Pet. 4:10-11

PRAYER OF APPLICATION:

4 - FOLLOWING GOD TO UNCOMFORTABLE PLACES

QUOTE from Chapter 3 — The "Sink or Swim" Method

Shortly before we moved to Ukraine, I wrote an enthusiastic letter to a friend, a former missionary. Laurie wrote back, "I remember how it is, you can't wait to get to the mission field; then you get there and wonder why you ever came." I dismissed the comment as part of her negative experience. I was sure I would never feel that way.

Two weeks after arrival in Ukraine, I wrote in my journal:

I'm covered with bug bites and my intestines churn. I'm tired of camping and want an indoor bathroom and a refrigerator. I can't even engage in small talk, much less expound the great truths of scripture to a lost and needy world. I feel as powerful and competent as a small piece of driftwood in the surf.

Why did we come anyway? We came because people in Ukraine are important to God. Jesus could have stayed in heaven where it was comfortable, but He left His place of privilege to come to this sin-sick world.

I feel helpless and don't like it. I can't talk to people, get to know them or express my desires. We can't find an apartment on our own and still don't know our way around town. We are dependent on other people to help us.

Though Jesus existed in the form of God, with all power, He came as a helpless baby. Did that helplessness frustrate Him? I don't think so. He was humble, willing to wait. Even as an adult, His power was limited—at least He limited the way He used it. He could have called legions of angels to ease His situation, but He didn't. (p.23)

CONNECT or REFLECT:

What was a time you felt "in over your head" and had to trust God for the outcome – or is there a way in which you feel overwhelmed now?

STUDY AND DISCUSS:
Obedience to God can put us into situations where we no longer feel in control. How can we accept these uncomfortable situations, instead of run away?

Summarize Phil. 2:5-8

Write down other Biblical examples where people were put in uncomfortable circumstances or situations "over their head" when they obeyed God.

Read and note: a) Who was called and how did they feel about it? And b) How did God reward their obedience?
a) Ex. 4:1-13, b) Ex. 14:30-31

a) Esther 4:9-16, b) Esther 9:1

a) Acts 18:9-10, b) 2 Tim. 4:17-18

a) Mat. 26:36-39, b) Phil. 2:8-11

How can we maintain a sense of sanity when we are in "over our head?"

What encouragement do the following scriptures give?
Ps. 18:1-3

Ps. 18:30-36

Ps. 62:5-8

Heb. 4:14-16

Heb. 12:1-3

PRAYER OF APPLICATION:

5 - FINDING JOY

QUOTE from Chapter 4 — Like a Trip to Disneyland:

As I lay in bed that night staring into the darkness, hot tears ran into my ears. I was so tired of simply coping with life, I couldn't imagine finding the energy needed to get that apartment livable.

Having grown up in the U.S., I was used to more options. Americans look at several houses before choosing one. I felt like a bride in a country where marriages are arranged. Such a bride has no choice—no choice but to choose her own happiness and to choose to make it work.

"God," I prayed, "I know that in Your presence is fullness of joy and at Your right hand are pleasures forever more. Help me find my peace in You. Help me make this new place a home and a place of peace."

The American pursuit of happiness is largely consumer oriented, I realized. Not happy? Then get a different brand, a different spouse, a new house, or more stuff. I remembered seeing a documentary film about Russian immigrants in the U.S. They felt overwhelmed by so many choices. In Russia, they didn't ask themselves if they are happy or not—they just did their best with the circumstances they had. I would have to learn to do the same.

I needed grace to get through this, I realized. God gives grace to the humble. Perhaps my point of pride is thinking I deserve to have life a bit more comfortable than the average Ukrainian. (p.31-32)

CONNECT or REFLECT:
What makes you happy?

STUDY AND DISCUSS:
Can you think of someone whose life radiates joy in spite of difficult circumstances? Briefly describe this person.

In what circumstances did Paul rejoice?
Col. 1:24

Phil. 2:17-18

Phil. 4:12

We can't always choose our circumstances, but we can choose our
attitude. In what types of difficulties are we told to rejoice? And why?
Mat. 5:11-12

Rom. 5:3-5

1 Pet. 1:6-9

2 Cor 4:17

Read. Phil. 4:4-7. How is it possible to "rejoice always?"

How do the following scriptures help answer this question?
Ps. 16:11

Ps. 31:7-8

Ps. 33:20-22

Ps 118:24

Hab. 3:17-19

2 Cor. 12:8-9

Luke 10:20

Read James 4:6 and write it in your own words.

Describe, if you can, an instance where humility helped you cope in a difficult circumstance.

PRAYER OF APPLICATION:

6 - RELATIONSHIPS AND MINISTRY

QUOTE from Chapter 5 — Garlic and Pig Fat:

Ukrainian housewives preserve produce in jars during the summer and fall for wintertime use. Wanting to learn how to can the Russian way, I visited Olga on one of her canning days. I helped her chop up eggplant, green peppers, and onions for some kind of vegetable relish. I never copied her recipe, but I enjoyed the fellowship and was eager to learn from her.

Cory brought variety to language studies by helping church members construct a Christian education wing. He hauled sand and rocks for cement while learning the Russian words for bucket, brick, and hurry up. He mixed cement by hand and dug trenches in the hard clay. Over lunch, he learned about "salo," slices of raw pig fat, served with bread and raw garlic cloves. He never developed a taste for salo but liked borscht.

Old women at the construction site had much advice for him. They told him not to work so hard. He should eat more. They rebuked him for whistling on the job since whistling brings poverty. He should carry bricks in a certain way. They didn't want to fill his bucket completely with mortar so it wouldn't be too heavy.

He got frequent comments on the white cotton socks he wore to work, since cotton was expensive in Ukraine and white socks were rare. He finally gave up trying to explain that those were his work socks and started wearing dark dress socks to the construction site.

"I don't even care that much about the building itself," he told me, "I just see it as a good way to build relationships." (p.39-41)

CONNECT or REFLECT:
Who was most instrumental in helping you in your decision to follow Christ?

STUDY AND DISCUSS:
How are relationships and the ability to build relationships essential for effective ministry?

What does Mat. 5:13-16 suggest in this regard?

What helps build strong relationships?

What hinders?

How do the following scriptures help answer these questions?
Gal. 5:13-14

Phil. 2:3-5

In Matthew 9, we find several instances in which Jesus ministered to different kinds of people in different circumstances. Identify them and note what we can learn from His example.
v. 2.

v. 9

vs. 10-13

vs. 18-19

vs. 20-22

vs. 35-36

Summarize: What do you learn from Jesus' example?

Consider the impact you can have on others. Make notes on the following verses.
Prov. 12:18

Prov. 18:21

Eph. 4:29

Col. 4:5-6

Prayerfully consider your circle of acquaintances. Name one or two you feel God would have you minister to in some way. What action should you take?

PRAYER OF APPLICATION:

7 – LEARNING TO BE CONTENT

QUOTE from Chapter 6 — Garage Sale Paradise

The door of one neighbor belonged to a young mother, Katya, who lived with her husband and their one-and-a-half-year old daughter. She had long, bleached-blond hair and wore skinny black leggings with platform shoes. She invited me to come visit sometime.

I wasn't sure when I should go, since she never suggested a day, but after several more vague invitations, I baked an applesauce cake and took it over.

She invited me in and motioned towards a bed-couch in her simple one-room apartment. Though her street clothes indicated she had money, her apartment told a different story. I sat on wet blankets, which smelled of urine. It's not "Russian" to use diapers, although I'd seen expensive, imported disposables at the market. Russian children more typically go through many changes of clothing.

I came home and thought how contentment depends on with whom you compare yourself. Our apartment was shabby and small by American standards, but a palace compared to our neighbors'. (p.49)

CONNECT or REFLECT:
If you could pick one thing you wish was different abut your life or circumstances, what would it be?

STUDY AND DISCUSS:
How do comparisons affect your sense of contentment?

How does contentment affect your ability to minister effectively?

If I had written 2 Cor. 12:10, I might have said, "I am content when I'm feeling strong, when people compliment me, when I'm successful, when people are nice to me, when life is easy." Read Paul's version. How could he be content with hardship? Look for clues in 2 Cor. 12:7-10.

Paul's trials and lifestyle gave him many opportunities for discontentment. Read his response in Phil. 4:10-13. What was his secret to contentment? What can we learn from his example?

How does Christ give strength for your response to this lesson's Connect and Reflect question?

How can we grow in our sense of contentment?

How do the following verses help answer this question?
1 Thes. 5:18

Phil. 4:8

1Tim. 6:6-11

Heb. 13:5-6

How can focusing on the needs of others help us to feel more content?

What do the following verses suggest in this regard?
Prov. 11:24-25

Luke 6:38

Prov. 14:21

PRAYER OF APPLICATION:

8 – PURIFICATION BY FIRE

QUOTE from Chapter 7 — Off the Pedestal

Those who think missionaries are "super saints" probably don't know any very well. Our new roles brought new kinds of stress, which like a refiner's fire, brought impurities to the surface. (p.53)

Some days, I woke up growling. I felt more angry, more often than I had in my whole life. I disliked the inconveniences, the sense of isolation, the language barrier, the hard work. I wondered, *will I ever feel at home?* Family, especially Cory, got the brunt of it.

I wrote in my journal: Some people believe in purgatory, the idea of getting cleaned up for heaven after death. I think God uses life to get us ready for Glory, to burn up the chaff so we can look and act like Jesus. I want to shine like gold, but I don't like the fire. (p.55)

CONNECT or REFLECT:
From what teacher did you learn the most while growing up?

STUDY AND DISCUSS:
What was a difficult experience that made you stronger? How did it strengthen you?

Of what value are hard times in our lives?
James 1:2-4

Job 23:10

1 Pet. 1:6-7

Rom. 5:3-5

2 Cor. 1:3-7

What is God's ultimate aim for our lives? (It's not our comfort!)

How do the following verses help answer this question?
Rom. 8:29

1 Pet. 2:21

1 Pet 1:7

QUOTE: "I used to think of God's calling as a place or profession. Now I see He isn't as concerned about the good we do for Him, as much as the good He can put in us. Obeying His call to a place or profession is a good way to prepare for corrective surgery." (p.53)

Do you agree or disagree? Why?

SURVIVING THE FIRE AS A COUPLE

QUOTE: When a couple heads to the mission field, it's like jumping into the deep end of a swimming pool when you don't know how to swim. It's hard to offer much support to your spouse while thrashing around trying to keep from going under. Someone advised us before we moved to Ukraine, "Give each other the freedom to struggle."

Nevertheless, I let each additional transgression build on and reinforce that firmly placed cornerstone, his failure to help me in the beginning like

I wanted. I focused on his faults so much I didn't see my own. His acts of kindness and words of affirmation bounced off my shell. Eventually, I found the freedom that results from forgiving your spouse for not being God. (p.54)

STUDY AND DISCUSS:

It is not uncommon to hear of couples who divorce after a time of crisis, for example, unemployment or the death of a child. How can you use times of stress to draw you closer together instead of drive you apart?

How can you apply Eph. 4:32 to your closest relationships?

Read 1 Cor. 13:4-7. Which characteristics of love can help you survive difficulties as a couple?

PRAYER OF APPLICATION:

9 - FEELING INADEQUATE

QUOTE from Chapter 8 — Walking in the Dark

Many years of propaganda made people suspicious of Christians. Christians were often suspicious of outsiders too—and anyone who attended church but didn't conform to their dress code.

In spite of the problems, we wanted to work with the existing church. We didn't want to start from scratch and didn't want to start an "American" church. We didn't want a program so dependent on us it would die if we left the country. Cory faithfully attended every church service in order to build relationships and gain insight into the church culture.

Walking home without streetlights from a candlelit church service— because the electricity was out—Cory reflected on how our time in Ukraine was like walking in the dark. "We barely know the language," he told me when he got home. "We don't know what's appropriate. We don't know when we are offending someone. We came with ideas of how we would like to help, but we are only beginning to see how complex the problems are and how much we really don't know." We needed Jesus to light our path. (p.63)

CONNECT or REFLECT:

What's something you are good at? A little-known talent?

STUDY AND DISCUSS:

Can you think of a time when God led you into a situation that seemed too big to handle? What happened?

In what way can a sense of inadequacy be a good thing?

How do the following verses help answer this question?
2 Cor. 1:8-11

2 Cor: 3:4-6

2 Cor. 4:7

2 Cor. 12:9-10

1 Cor. 1:26-31

1 Cor. 2:1-5

Acts 4:13

What should we do when we feel inadequate in our work or ministry?

What do the following verses suggest?
Jn. 15:4-5

James 1:5

2 Tim. 3:16-17

What encouragement does Prov. 2:1-11 give?

In what area do you need God to be strong in your weakness?

PRAYER OF APPLICATION:

10 - WHAT IF MINISTRY ISN'T "FUN?"

QUOTE from Chapter 9 — Rat Hats and Cough Syrup

Cold wind blew through the cracks around our window frames. Mid-December, I finally stuffed paper in the openings to block out some of the wind. Lacking hot water, washing hands or working at the kitchen sink numbed my fingers. The water went off all over the city for several days because of a broken pipe. Though I always kept some water on hand, that time it wasn't enough.

An icy fog hung over the city during the winter so it was useless to hang laundry outside. Clothes didn't dry; they simply absorbed the smell of coal smoke. I draped laundry all over the house, which contributed to a problem of condensation. Water dripped from the kitchen ceiling and our wallpaper mildewed.

I wondered, *what are we doing here, going through all this discomfort?* I looked forward to the completion of our four-year term so we could get back to "normal living." Then I read 2 Corinthians 5, and I remembered why we came.

Cory said, "A lot of people ask me, 'What do you like best here?'" He shook his head. "What is there to like? I keep thinking, what are we doing here? It takes so much energy just to survive and the task is so daunting."

A few days later, he told me at breakfast, "I had a strange dream last night. I went to a place with the best conditions possible for a missionary. I could even go fishing and play basketball. I was on an island that had everything you could ever want for making life comfortable, but there weren't any indigenous people! As soon as I arrived, I knew I'd made a mistake."

He took another bite of pancake. "I'm reading the book, *In His Steps*. The ultimate question is, 'What would Jesus do?' The challenge to live for Jesus—even if it involves sacrifice—appeals to me. That's why I wanted to come to Ukraine. Serving Him is hard, but it gives purpose to life." (p.69-70)

CONNECT or REFLECT:

If health or money was not an issue and you had no other responsibilities, where would you go for vacation, or what would you do?

STUDY AND DISCUSS:
What criteria should we use for deciding how to spend our time or live our lives? Would it be whether the activity gives us pleasure? Or does it depend on a sense of call? Is there a place for both? Explain.

What should you do if you feel called to do something that isn't fun?

Read the following passages. What guidelines do they give for setting priorities for our lives?
2 Cor. 5:9,14-20

Eph. 5:1-2

Phil. 2:3-8

1 Pet. 2:21

Rom. 12:1-2

Rom. 14:7-8

1 Cor. 6:19-20

1 Cor. 9:24-27

How is the Christian life like a race? What things slow you down? Heb. 12:1-3

How can we encourage others who are struggling?

How can we find encouragement for ourselves?

PRAYER OF APPLICATION:

11- DEALING WITH DEPRESSION

QUOTE from Chapter 10 — No Old Man on a Cloud
One member of the team from Kansas joined me in the kitchen after dinner. She watched me heat water on the stove and kept me company while I washed dishes.

"How do you live here?" she asked. "Do you like it? Or, ah, are you content? Maybe that's a better way to put it."

Fair question—how should I answer? "I guess feelings don't have anything to do with it," I said finally. "We are here because we are supposed to be. Some days, it's hard to get out of bed to a cold house, but the girls need to eat breakfast. I need to shop. I need to cook and clean. We need to study Russian so we can understand what's going on around us."

I told her I often thought of a devotional I'd read by Elisabeth Elliot. She said that people often focus too much on how they feel, instead of simply doing what they need to do in spite of how they feel. By simply "doing the next thing," she walked her way out of many pits of despair. Following her philosophy helped me cope. (p.87-88)

CONNECT or REFLECT:
What gets you out of bed in the morning?

STUDY AND DISCUSS:
God gave us the ability to feel emotion. To what extent should we pay attention to our feelings?

Read the following scriptures. Who was depressed? Why? What was God's solution?
Gen 21:14-19

Num 11:10-17

Jonah 4:5-10

Read Psalms 73. It begins with the dark thoughts of a depressed man. He receives new perspective in God's presence. What are his final conclusions?

How can we overcome depression—or continue to operate in times of depression?

What encouragement or advice do the following scriptures give?
Ps. 42:11

Ps. 9:9-10

Is. 26:3-4

Is. 40:26-31

Ps. 40:1-5

Paul gives two prescriptions for peace in Phil. 4:6-9. What are they? vs. 6-7

vs. 8-9

PRAYER OF APPLICATION:

12 - WHAT HAS GREATEST VALUE?

QUOTE from Chapter 11 — He is Risen Indeed

While Cory took over child-care, I headed to a retreat for missionary women in Odessa. We stayed at a former campground for Young Pioneers, a Communist club. Though not great, the facilities were adequate and located on the beach. About thirty women gathered from different parts of Ukraine. I enjoyed worship in English, pizza, and fellowship with women from my culture.

We went to Ukraine for the people of Ukraine, but it takes a lot of work to build relationships cross-culturally. It goes beyond trying to communicate in a new language. I wondered if I was doing something offensive. Was I dressed okay? Was I smiling too much? I could relax when spending time with those who play the relationship game with the same set of rules.

The speaker talked about Abraham's walk with God. God required sacrifices of Abraham but blessed him along the way. She encouraged the women to list things they have given up.

Ideas flowed freely: family, friends, ability to communicate, comforts, adequate health care. Some told stories with an edge of resentment.

As I looked at my list of "things sacrificed," I realized I haven't truly surrendered those things until I could say with Paul, "I consider everything like rubbish compared to the surpassing value of knowing Christ." (p. 97-98)

CONNECT or REFLECT:

As a child, what did you want to do or be when you grew up?

STUDY AND DISCUSS:

Luke 9:23 indicates that following Jesus includes sacrifice. In what ways has obedience to God required sacrifice from you?

Read Phil. 3:4-11. What did Paul sacrifice? Also check 2 Cor. 11:23-28.

How do we get to the place of Paul, where the things we value are like rubbish compared to the value of knowing Christ?

Do you think his shift in values came instantly or over time?

What is of greatest value according to Jer. 9:23-24?

What does it mean to "know God" or "know Christ?"

How does knowledge of God affect other areas of life?

How do the following verses answer that question?
1 Jn. 2:3-6

2 Pet. 1:2-3

How does knowledge of God increase our willingness to make sacrifices for His sake?

Read Phil. 3:7-14 again. Make notes on how knowledge of Christ affected other areas of Paul's life.

2 Pet. 3:18 says we are to "grow in the grace and knowledge of our Lord and Savior, Jesus Christ." How do we grow in our knowledge of Christ?

PRAYER OF APPLICATION:

13 - My Cross and His

QUOTE from Chapter 12 — Bitter Water Made Sweet

I woke up one morning with a thought out of nowhere. No, it must have been from God. *When the people of Israel came to bitter water, Moses did something so they could drink it. What did he do?*

I lay there for a moment to ponder. Did he hit it with his rod? Or throw salt in it, or a branch? I didn't have time to look it up, so while making breakfast and going to the market and canning cherries, I wondered. I thought of circumstances I didn't like, situations that made life in Ukraine hard to swallow. I made a mental list. What was God trying to say? Could He still turn bitter water into sweet?

While the girls napped, I looked it up. Exodus 15:25: "Then he cried out to the Lord, and the Lord showed him a tree; and he threw it into the waters, and the waters became sweet."

I thought of another tree, the cross of Jesus. I wrote down everything I didn't like in Ukraine and thought, *How does the cross apply to this? Can the cross make my bitter waters sweet?*

-Inconveniences: It wasn't convenient for Christ to leave heaven and die for us.

-Sporadic water: Jesus said, "I thirst."

-Crowds at the market: Jesus died for them.

-Carrying heavy bags home from the market: Jesus carried a cross.

-Language barrier: Jesus left a position of power to become a helpless baby.

-The dirt and smells: Jesus left a place of beauty for a sin-ruined world. He walked dusty roads and lived in cities without indoor plumbing.

-Separation from family: Jesus was separated from the Father, so we might have fellowship.

-Mundane housework: Jesus was homeless.

-Some don't accept us: Not everyone liked Jesus.

I knew Jesus called us to pick up our cross to follow Him, but decided I should focus more on the cross of Christ instead of my own. Jesus suffered more than I ever will.

Jesus had a bitter cup to drink too, but for the joy set before Him, He endured the cross. He didn't focus on His misery but on the reason why He went through it all—people. *Lord, give me a greater love for people.*

I saw two sides to the cross: His suffering and His love. He loves people in general, but He also loves *me*. When Jesus commanded us to "Go into all the world and preach the Gospel," He promised to be with us until the very end. (p.103-104)

CONNECT or REFLECT:
What beverage do you dislike?

STUDY AND DISCUSS:
Read Heb.12:1-6. Paraphrase verse 3.

How does meditation on Christ and his suffering give us strength?

Study verse 2. How does it help answer the last question?

Creator God took on flesh (Mat. 1:23). What difference does that make to us?

How does Heb. 4:14-16 help answer this question?

List some areas of personal difficulty. Note how Christ can sympathize with each, or how His situation was even worse. For help in comparing your suffering with His, read Is. 53.

Note key phrases in the following verses:
Luke 9:23

Mat. 11:28-30

Considering Mat. 11:28-30, what makes our cross lighter?

PRAYER OF APPLICATION:

14 - GIFTS OF GRACE

QUOTE from Chapter 13 — Now What?

I stood at the sink washing dishes under a trickle of water and listed reasons why I didn't like being a missionary in Ukraine. It was just a partial list, since it would take too long to review everything. Stress on the family. Cory hadn't found any fulfilling ministry. Separation from loved ones. Inconveniences. Unexpected outages of water and electricity. The sense of being out of control. I missed the "normal life" where you get what you earn.

The sound of the television interrupted my thoughts. The girls were watching a video, a gift from someone we had never met. It made me think of other blessings. Our new water filter was another gift and it gave us clean drinking water that no longer tasted like swamp. Our monthly financial report recorded the generosity of so many. We were privileged to have daily prayer support. We did nothing to earn these gifts; and we had no way to repay.

Gifts of grace. Grace is something you don't earn—can't earn. It goes beyond salvation. We had health. Adequate food. A good car. We had friends who loved us, in Ukraine and abroad. Stefan gave us a gunnysack of potatoes and wouldn't accept payment. Anya earned just $40 a month, but often bought treats for Janelle and Alicia. I felt humbled by their generosity.

"Normal" folks get what they earn. They have their feet squarely on the ground and feel some sense of control. Living by faith has me dangling from a parachute or a hot-air balloon—or something up there—no, Someone. The cord is strong and when I'm grateful, the view is fine.

I stood at the sink and listed my gifts of grace. Only a partial list, for it would take too long to list everything. (p.113)

CONNECT or REFLECT:

What was a memorable gift you received, not necessarily expensive?

STUDY AND DISCUSS:
Do you find it easier to focus on life's difficulties or on the blessings?
Explain.

Read the following verses and list some of God's gracious gifts to us,
blessings we could never earn. A conservative count uncovered 30
blessings in these verses. How many do you find?
1 Jn. 4:10

Eph. 2:1-9

Eph. 1:3-14

Eph. 1:18-20

Ps. 103

James 1:17

Reviewing this list of blessings, which one is the most meaningful to you? Why?

List other good things in your life.

PRAYER OF APPLICATION:

15 - PURSUIT OF HAPPINESS OR SOMETHING ELSE?

QUOTE from Chapter 14 — Hope Endures

I read the book, *Christy*, about a sheltered nineteen-year-old girl who moved to the Appalachian Mountains to teach in a mission school. Culture shock set in. Appalled by the dirt, poverty and strange customs, she said that maybe her parents were right and she didn't belong there.

The Quaker missionary told her she would never see the terrible side of life in sheltered ivory towers. Was she supposed to be there or was she just running away from home? Everyone has something good to contribute, but if she didn't do the work that was hers to do, it may never get done.

I didn't know what we'd ever contribute in Ukraine, but I wanted to persevere until God moved us on to something else. (p.120)

I remembered the group of American musicians who performed in our town the previous year. Their testimonies all followed the line: "I wanted happiness so I tried this and that, but I wasn't happy until I tried Jesus." I never heard, "I was a sinner and Jesus forgave my sin." Happiness is fleeting, but hope endures.

It seems most Americans think "pursuit of happiness" is the ultimate goal in life. After all, it's in our Constitution, so isn't it our divine right—especially if we are good Christians?

While criticizing shallow-thinking Americans, I have to look in the mirror. I've had the notion if I obey God, I'll be truly fulfilled—but running the race isn't always fun or fulfilling. God blesses His children, but sometimes I have to hang in there as an act of endurance—not for the blessing, but because God deserves it. (p.116)

CONNECT or REFLECT:
What initially attracted you to Christianity?

STUDY AND DISCUSS:

Is it legitimate to say, "If you want happiness, follow Jesus?" Why or why not?

What did Jesus promise his followers?

Jn. 5:24

Jn. 7:37-39

Jn. 10:10

Jn. 15:18-21

Mat. 10:24-25

Mat. 10:34-39

Jn. 16:33

Jn. 14:27

Mat. 28:20

What do you hope to gain from your choice to follow Jesus?

Other than personal benefit, for what reason should we follow Jesus?

How do the following scriptures help answer this question?
Rev. 4:11

Rev. 5:12

PRAYER OF APPLICATION:

16 - ENCOUNTERING OPPOSITION

QUOTE from Chapter 15 — We Battle Not Against Flesh and Blood

Tatiana told us of a news report she had seen on television. They showed footage of open graves in the Simferopol cemetery and said that foreign missionaries were to blame for the spread of Satan worship. The report quoted government authorities as saying they need tighter controls on giving visas to foreigners. "Though not all encourage Satan worship, they cause conflict with our own churches."

When we talked to Stefan about the news report and brochure put out by the Orthodox Church, he said, "This is nothing compared to what we faced during the 1970's. They accused us of terrible things. They took our children from us."

Still, it felt strange to us to be called "the enemy." We are nice people. I had always skimmed over Jesus' words, "Don't be surprised when people hate you" since I never experienced it before. (p.124)

Some think adversity and the presence of adversaries means the door is closed. Paul, however, wrote to the Corinthians, "a wide door of effective service has been opened to me, and there are many adversaries" (1 Cor.16:9 NAS). One can have fruitful ministry in spite of opposition. (p.125)

CONNECT or REFLECT:

Can you recall an instance when you faced opposition for doing what you felt was right? What happened?

STUDY AND DISCUSS:

How *should* we respond to opposition?

Read the following scriptures. Note the main characters and how they responded to opposition.
Acts 4:13,21-31

Acts 5:17-29

Acts 5:40-42

Because we like to be liked, we are tempted to "hide our light" or "lose our flavor as salt" (Mat. 5:13-16) in order to avoid conflict. What do the following verses promise?
2 Tim. 3:12

Mat. 5:11-12

Mat. 10:18-20

What advice do the following scriptures give for times of opposition? Note actions and attitudes.
1 Jn: 4:4-11

1 Pet. 3:8-17

1 Pet. 4:12-19

1 Pet. 5:7-10

Eph. 6:10-18

Luke 6:27-28

Rom. 12:17-21

PRAYER OF APPLICATION:

17 - HANDLING HARDSHIP

QUOTE from Chapter 16 — Our Tiny Flame

While visiting churches in the U.S. for three months, many people asked us, "So, how do you like it over there?"

It's a normal question. I thought a well-adjusted missionary should be able to say, "Oh, I've never felt so fulfilled in all my life." Or at least, "It's rewarding, in spite of the difficulties."

I could only reply, "It's a difficult place to live, but that's where we feel God wants us for now." I decided that wasn't a lesser answer.

How did Moses like leading the Israelites? Did Paul enjoy getting beat up and shipwrecked? If you had asked Jesus, "So, how do you like living on earth?" what would He have said?

They all had a mission to accomplish. It would have been easier for Jesus to stay in heaven—"but for the joy set before Him, He endured the cross."

Likewise, in Hebrews 11, the "faith chapter," men and women chose to do difficult things, not for immediate reward, but in faith that something good would result.

We enjoyed church services in English during furlough and felt as though we hadn't worshiped for almost two years. One sermon, however, put worship in another context. The pastor quoted King David's words, "I will not offer to God something which costs me nothing." Sacrifice is an act of worship.

I realized worship isn't simply meaningful songs, inspiring sermons, and close fellowship. Worship includes, "Jesus, I do this for you as an act of love and out of appreciation for your supreme sacrifice for me." Unfortunately, I usually focus on the cost more than Christ. (p.133-134)

CONNECT or REFLECT:

Of people you personally know, who stands out in your mind as a great person of faith?

STUDY AND DISCUSS:
Read Heb. 11 and list difficult things done by men and women of faith.

What was the result of their faith? Heb. 11:2,6

List trials Paul endured, recorded in 2 Cor. 6:4-10

In spite of his many problems, what was Paul's frame of mind? Note key words in 2 Cor. 6:10 and 2 Cor. 4:1,7-11

What enabled Paul to endure hardship? Note key phrases in 2 Cor. 4:16-18

When facing hardship, what helps you through it?

What can you glean from the following verses that can help you during difficulty?
Jer. 17:7-8

Ps. 18:1-3

Ps. 18:30-36

Ps. 46:1-3,10-11

Ps. 57:1-3

Rom. 8:31-39

1 Cor. 10:13

PRAYER OF APPLICATION:

18 - SELF-PRESERVATION OR SACRIFICE?

QUOTE from Chapter 17 — "Always Ready"
Along with the other children in her first grade class, Anya was inducted into the "Octoberists," a club named after the October revolution. In a solemn ceremony, older children gave first graders red metal pins that pictured Lenin as a child.

At age ten, she eagerly joined the next level, Pioneer Club. "I remember feeling so proud when they gave me my red scarf," she recalled.

Communist leaders told school children that the red in the scarf was like a little piece of their flag. The red in the flag stood for the blood of those who died in the October revolution. "You too, must be ready to give your life for your country."

All children learned the story of young Pavel Morozov. After the revolution, communist leaders required all citizens to give their cattle and land to state cooperatives. One "rich and greedy" man didn't want to share with others, so his son, Pavel Morozov, reported him to the authorities. The father was arrested. Pavel's uncle and brother took little Pavel to a field and beat him until he died. What a hero.

"We should be brave like Pavel and do what is right for our country," teachers told the children.

When Pioneer Club rallies were held at the statue of Lenin, the leader would say, "Are you ready to fight for the Communist party?"

The young Pioneers saluted with right arms raised at a slant over their heads. "Always ready!" they replied in unison. Anya explained that the salute signified readiness from the top of the head to the bottom of the feet. (p.137-138)

CONNECT or REFLECT:
In what way did you see your parents (or those who raised you) sacrifice for you?

STUDY AND DISCUSS:
Soon after we arrived in Ukraine, a missionary told us, "Be careful or they will suck the life out of you!" What advice would you give a missionary or pastor or young mother or anyone else who serves?

Consider Eph. 6:10

1 Pet. 4:11

Ex. 20:8

Devout Communists. Suicide bombers. Terrorists. Throughout the world and throughout history, we find people willing to die for a cause. Our first instinct is self-preservation. Note Biblical examples of those willing to sacrifice themselves. What motivated them?
Ex. 32:31-32

Dan. 3:16-18

Dan. 6:10-12

Jn. 10:11-18

What was Paul's attitude toward self-sacrifice? Note main phrases in the following verses.
Rom. 9:2-3

Phil. 2:17

2 Cor. 12:15

Acts 21:10-13

Acts 20:22-24

What do we risk from pursuing self-preservation? Mat.16:25

How can we become more like the godly characters cited above?

How do the following scriptures help answer this question?
Jn. 15:9-13

1 Jn. 3:16

Rom. 12:1

2 Cor. 8:5

Phil. 4:13

PRAYER OF APPLICATION:

19 - MAKING DISCIPLES

QUOTE from Chapter 18 — Our Second Summer

My sister wrote to say that her girls missed playing with my girls when they visited Grandma's house. I read the letter to Janelle and Alicia.

"Will we see them again when we go to Grandma's house?" Alicia asked. "But then we will be too big to play. We will be mamas then." When you are not quite four, two more years seems like forever.

Five-year old Janelle said, "You have to be really old when you get married. I'm going to get married when I am ten."

They discussed the size of Stefan's family. "They have five children," noted Janelle. "I wonder how Stefan and Nadia take care of them."

Alicia suggested, "Maybe they brush their teeth by themselves."

At one time, I wondered if my babies would ever become potty trained. They grew older and I wondered if they would ever learn to tie their shoes. Then, it clicked and they spent the rest of the day looking for shoes and strings they could use for practice.

Cory came home that evening and reported on the brothers' meeting. "Igor says they should be more careful who they baptize this year, since most of the people baptized last year no longer attend."

Cory thought the problem wasn't with the new converts but with poor "parenting." He later preached on the topic of discipleship. He compared new Christians to babies. Parents don't expect babies to cook, wash clothes, and figure out everything alone. Parents spend a lot of time caring for the new member of the family. He stressed that all believers are to "go and make disciples"—it's not just the job of the pastor or church leaders. (p.146)

CONNECT or REFLECT:

Who influenced you most in your Christian growth? How did they help you?

STUDY AND DISCUSS:
What do the following scriptures show about stages of spiritual growth?
Heb. 5:12-14

1 John 2:12-14

Col. 2:6-7

How can we promote spiritual growth in others? How did others help you in your spiritual growth?

What principles do the following verses suggest for helping others grow spiritually?
1 Thes. 2:7-8

1 Thes. 2:10-12

Col. 1:28-29

Mat. 28:19-20

1 Cor. 13:1-2

Mark 12:30-31

1 Cor. 11:1

Col. 1:9-12   For what did Paul pray? What was the goal?

Read Eph. 4:11-16 and look for objectives or goals when making disciples. List them.

PRAYER OF APPLICATION:

20 - CONFLICT WITH OTHER CHRISTIANS

QUOTE from Chapter 19 — "Don't Worry, It Will Get Worse"
I grew up hearing stories about the persecuted church behind the Iron Curtain. I thought Russian Christians must be as close to sainthood as you can get. I often heard, "The best thing that could happen to American churches is the purifying fire of persecution." I moved behind the former Iron Curtain and learned Russian believers aren't perfect either.

Believers in the Soviet Union had lived with self-preservation as their focus for so long, the church had a hard time breaking out of that mindset. In the absence of Bibles, preachers taught traditions. Spirituality was often judged by conformity to external things such as head coverings, simple dress, and a certain hairstyle. Church members viewed outsiders with suspicion. (p.147)

Cory, Andre, and Stefan continued to meet to discuss how they might train people to plant churches. Andre felt they needed many new churches around Crimea. Cory reminded him the existing churches would feel threatened by new churches. "Some people will criticize no matter what you do," Andre said. (p.148)

Andre was widely respected by church leaders in the region; at least he had the respect of most. When he told Igor about the plans for training church planters, Igor accused him of meeting in secret and said, "You need to get advice from those with more experience."

Andre said, "I'm listening."

Igor criticized Andre, Stefan, and Cory at length. He said Andre and Stefan were chasing American money. They were traitors. Stefan was lazy. Andre wanted to take over as pastor. Cory was a traitor too. He was supposed to help the church but worked against it instead. He didn't understand the culture or respect Ukrainian church traditions.

After that meeting, Andre told Cory, "We have a Russian saying, 'Don't worry, it will get worse.'" (p.152)

CONNECT or REFLECT:
What did your parents do when you quarreled with siblings? If you had no siblings, who did you quarrel with the most?

STUDY AND DISCUSS:
How has criticism helped you?

Even when it's not given properly, God can use criticism to correct us, to give us wisdom. Can you think of Biblical examples where criticism or conflict was necessary or produced a better outcome? If so, what happened?

Make notes on the following examples:
2 Sam. 12:1-14

Gal. 2:11-14

We rarely welcome correction. What do the following verses say?
Prov. 13:10

Prov. 15:31-33

Can you think of Biblical examples where the person being criticized was right to ignore the criticism? If so, what happened?

Make notes on the following examples:
Ex. 16:2-3

Num. 12:1-2

Mat. 16:21-23

Acts 5:26-29

Acts 11:2-18

2 Cor. 10:8-11

How do we know if we should heed or ignore the criticism?

How do the following verses help answer this question?
2 Tim. 3:16-17

John 16:7-13

Prov. 2:1-11

Prov. 11:14

What advice would you give someone facing conflict with co-workers, family members, or other Christians?

Note words of advice given in the following scriptures.
Col. 3:12-15

Heb.12:14-15

Rom. 12:17-21

In what ways would peace with others depend on you?

Under what circumstances would peaceful relationships not depend on you?

How should we correct those needing correction?

Note key phrases in the following verses:
Prov. 12:18

Prov. 18:13

Gal. 6:1

PRAYER OF APPLICATION:

21- MY WILL OR GOD'S?
MAKING DECISIONS

QUOTE from Chapter 20 — Thankful for Candles

I enjoyed my tour of Kiev and stayed up late that night talking to Vicky. "It has been a lot harder for us to live in Ukraine than we expected," I told her from my mattress on the floor of her room. "Our mission organization wants to know if we plan to come back for another term, but we don't know what to tell them."

I described our living conditions, then said, "For a while, I thought, 'I'll complete this term, so we can save face with our supporters, but I won't come back to Ukraine again. I don't even care or want to know what God thinks about it.' That sounded unspiritual, so I changed it to: 'I'll come back if God gives me the desire to come back.' That sounds safe enough, since I can't imagine getting the desire. I am able to live here, but I don't like living here. It's hard."

"Is there something else you feel God is calling you to do?" Vicky asked.

"No, I just want a nicer house and an easier lifestyle. It's hard being so far from my family, especially with children who grow up so fast without getting to see grandparents and cousins."

"Does Cory like it here?"

"No. It's hard for him, too."

Vicky admitted she didn't have many answers for me. "On one hand, I know God is a shepherd who takes care of His sheep. On the other hand, I know God sometimes asks us to do difficult things. I don't think you can make a decision based on whether or not something is hard. God knows how much you can handle and He can make up for the difference."

The trip to Kiev gave me food for thought in the following weeks. I had seen caves where monks hid from the world and suffered, it seemed, just for the sake of suffering. Why couldn't I accept hardship with joy when my journey to the world included suffering for the sake of Christ?

I later jotted in my journal:

"...they first gave themselves to the Lord and to us by the will of God" (2 Cor. 8:5). It's of no value to simply give ourselves to the work of the Lord. We must give ourselves to the Lord first, and then to whatever, wherever He directs.

Lord, I don't know how else to give myself to You. I don't want to run from this place out of personal dislike, or stay out of a misguided sense of duty. I can only put myself in Your hands. I want my roots to go deep into Your water of life so I might not wither in this dry land. Do you have anything to say, Lord?

I wanted a sense of whether or not we should return to Ukraine. The only thought which came to mind, however, was: *I love you...and My plans for you are for a future and a hope.* I realized God was more interested in my relationship with Him, than what I did for Him. I continued to write:

I've been like a child who drags her feet and screams, "I don't want to go!" That alone takes so much energy. I'd rather walk willingly and peacefully by Your side, holding Your hand, and trusting You will carry me in the places that are too difficult for me. You are big enough to carry me, and You love me enough to do that. (p.158-160)

CONNECT or REFLECT:
In what way do you need God's guidance or want to know His will?

STUDY AND DISCUSS:
God promises to guide us. Make notes on the following scriptures.
Jn. 10:27

Is. 30:21

Ps. 32:8-9

What factors can hinder our ability to hear God's leading?

How might we improve our ability to hear God's leading?

Read these verses, noting actions or attitudes that can improve our ability to hear God's leading.
Ezek. 18:29-32

Is. 50:4-5

Jer. 42:6

Prov. 3:5-6

If timing is an issue, if God isn't ready to show us the next step, what can we do? Make notes on the following verses:
Is. 50:10

Ps. 33:20-22

Ps. 37:3-5

How much we trust God affects our willingness to follow Him. What do the following verses show about God's intentions for us?
Ps. 84:11

Jer. 29:11

Jer. 7:23

Ps. 25:8-10

List the various ways the Lord, our Shepherd, cares for us.
Is. 40:11

Ps. 23

What can we expect when we trust God and follow His leading?
Ps. 16:11

Ps. 34:4-10

Ps. 84:11-12

Is. 58:11

Rom. 8:28

PRAYER OF APPLICATION:

22 - SURVIVING STRESS

QUOTE from Chapter 21 — Heart Trouble

Late in December, Anya walked to church with us. She had missed quite a few Sundays and cried during most of our twenty-minute walk to church. "It's like when a child gets hurt visiting the doctor," she said. "After that, he starts screaming whenever he sees a white coat. I feel that way about church. I had no peace in the world and thought I would find it in church. But there is no peace, no love. It's cold."

I prayed with her. She seemed prepared by the time we reached the church building, but she left early, crying. Like someone with a fresh sunburn, it didn't take much for a painful reaction.

Anya came to our house a few days later. She didn't look good—a little pale, a little nervous.

"My heart is acting up," she said. "I wanted to be near a phone in case I need to call an ambulance. Stress makes my heart worse so a doctor gave me permission to stay home from work. I'm back now, but I still feel nervous around people, paranoid.

I got our Russian Bible and asked her read the verses in Philippians 4 about thinking on what is good. I turned to 2 Corinthians. Paul said he was afflicted, but not crushed. "When you are filled up with the love of God," I said, "you won't get crushed when people step on you. Like a box, I can crush it only if it's empty." (p.163-164)

When Cory came home, he said, "I have that tightness in my chest again. My heartbeat is irregular, too. Here, feel my pulse." Sure enough, his pulse felt irregular to me, too. A doctor examined Cory later and concluded he had a stress-induced arrhythmia.

Cory had been under a lot of stress. He found church politics even more difficult than cultural adjustments and language learning. Tensions continued with Igor. Cory tried to work things out with him, but received a hostile response. The church planters' training program seemed like a good idea, but that too faced opposition and so many things could go wrong.

Cory started walking along the waterfront every morning and used the time for prayer and praise. It helped. He also decided to cut back on activities at the church and focus his energy on developing the training program. (p.161-162)

CONNECT or REFLECT:
What is your favorite way to relax?

STUDY AND DISCUSS:
What are some sources of stress in your life.

Stress is part of life. The Bible records many examples of people under stress. Can you think of anyone in the Bible who faced the same kind of stress that affects you? List three Biblical characters facing stressful circumstances. How did they respond? What did God do?

Read the following scriptures. Note the character, the source of stress, and God's solution.
Ex. 18:13-24

1 Kings 3:5-14

1 Kings 17:10-16

1 Kings 19:1-7

Mark 6:30-46

2 Cor. 7:5-7

How do you think God wants you to respond to the sources of stress in your life?

Read the following verses, noting our part and God's part.
Ps. 46:10-11

Isaiah 43:1-2

Ps. 57:1-2

Jn. 14:27

Mat 6:31-34

PRAYER OF APPLICATION:

23 - FINDING REST: LAYING LOADS AT HIS FEET

QUOTE from Chapter 22 — Training Program Begins

The question of whether or not we should sign up for another term in Ukraine continued to hang over my head. Cory and I discussed it often.

"I don't like it here most of the time either," he said. "It seems like God is using us though. But I couldn't do it without you. If you don't want to come back, we won't come back. We're in this together."

"I don't know," I said. "We still have a few more months before we have to decide. I guess we'll know when we need to know." I wrote in my journal:

> I can hang on for eighteen more months, but the thought of coming here again feels so depressing. What would we do in the U.S.? I don't know. I just want to be some place where life isn't so hard physically, socially, spiritually, and emotionally. Ultimately, heaven is the only place we will no longer have pain or problems.

> Before we came to Ukraine, I told supporting churches, "We have all of eternity to be comfortable. I want my brief life to count for something of eternal value." That is still true—I just want an easier road. What's your perspective, Lord?

> *"Come unto me, all who are weary and heavy-laden and I will give you rest. Take My yoke upon you and learn from Me, for I am gentle and humble in heart; and you will find rest for your soul. For My yoke is easy, and My load is light."*

> I come, with burdens of loneliness, sadness. I confess I think your attitude is, "Come to me and I will give you more to carry." But you say, "Come to me when you are carrying too much and I will give you rest." What are we carrying that you don't intend for us to carry? I know we are supposed to be here for now. So what are we not supposed to carry?

> Concern for the future and for our health. Anxiety for the welfare of the girls. Concern about our effectiveness. I dump my load at your feet. (p.171-172)

CONNECT or REFLECT:

What was a "restful" place you have been?

STUDY AND DISCUSS:
Ever since the time of Adam and Eve, Satan has tried to cast doubts on the goodness of God's character. Have you ever suspected God would make your life more difficult if you gave Him free reign in your life? If so, what was the situation?

Read and paraphrase Mat. 11:28-30

Can you identify any area or areas where you feel "weary or heavy-laden?" If so, in what way?

Jesus promises to give us rest. What is the relationship between trusting God and finding rest?

How do the following verses help answer that question?
Heb. 3:19, 4:1-3

Is. 26:3-4

What is God's attitude toward us and our burdens?
1 Pet. 5:7

Ps. 103:13-14

Is. 30:18

Read and note what assistance God provides and when He provides it.
Ps. 55:22

Phil. 4:6-7

Ps. 68:19-20

Read and paraphrase Ps. 139:23-24

Prayerfully consider — are you carrying something you are not supposed
to carry? With God's help, identify it and lay it down.

PRAYER OF APPLICATION:

24 - GOD'S STRENGTH
IN OUR WEAKNESS

QUOTE from Chapter 23 — Village Visit

All winter, I had anticipated the arrival of my sister, Linda, and her husband, Mike, who hoped to adopt two little boys from Ukraine. While waiting for their train in Simferopol, I saw several street kids, around ten years old, sniffing glue from plastic bags. A missionary who worked with such kids told me that many of them earned money for glue through prostitution. Many children who grow up in state-run "orphanages" end up on the street when they are old enough to run away.

Mike and Linda obtained permission to adopt from a large children's home and chose two little boys. Few children at the home were actually orphans—typically, their mothers abandoned them at maternity hospitals at birth.

The adoption process was a lengthy ordeal. After standing in lines all day one day without accomplishing anything, they came home feeling very discouraged and frustrated with the system. The smells of the crowd plus the sense of despair, hostility, and oppression seemed overwhelming.

"You just want to get out of there, and you don't care what else happens," said Mike.

I understood. We also had experienced the sense of "what did we get ourselves into." On the positive side, when feeling helpless we came to realize that if anything good would ever happen, God must get all the credit. (p.180)

CONNECT or REFLECT:

Have you ever seen a rescue, needed to be rescued, or been the rescuer? What happened? (Ie. burning building, near drowning, stranded?)

STUDY AND DISCUSS:
The Bible often shows how God's intervention made all the difference in situations where success, protection, or provision would have been humanly impossible. Write down several examples.

From these scriptures note the situation, what God did, and any words of encouragement or statements of faith we can apply.
Gen. 18:10-14

2 Chron. 20:1-4,13-23

2 Chron. 32:1-8,16-22

Luke 1:34-38

Luke 8:49-56

2 Cor. 4:7-10, 16-18

Thinking that a successful outcome is dependant on us can be stressful. Note how God works in spite of our weakness.
Zech. 4:6

Ps. 37:5-7

Ps. 37:23-26

Ps. 59:16-17

Ps. 138:7-8

Jer. 17:5-8

Jer. 32:17

2 Cor. 3:4-6

2 Cor. 12:9-10

As God leads into circumstances where you can't control the outcome, you do the possible and trust God for the impossible. Are you in a situation where success depends on God's intervention? What can you do? What is God's part?

PRAYER OF APPLICATION:

25 - FACING FEAR

QUOTE from Chapter 24 — Camp and the KGB

The intelligence office, formerly known as the KGB, left a message for Stefan, saying they wanted to meet with him. Stefan called the office and told them that if they want to see him, they could come to the church to talk to him. "I am here every Sunday morning."

He told Cory, "I know their tactics. They like to get you off in an office by yourself." During the Soviet times, they harassed Stefan constantly.

They called on Stefan again. He came to our house after the meeting and told us about it. The agent had asked him about the camp, about the training center, and about us.

We found this interest from the KGB unnerving, having grown up with more freedom and privacy. One person told us, "I'm one hundred percent sure the KGB listens to your phone conversations." We heard from other Americans in Crimea that their e-mail was not secure.

Though we thought of ourselves as ordinary folk, we were the only foreigners in town. Apparently, they were suspicious of our motives. We had heard that some people thought we were spies—why else would Americans come to this backwater town with poor living conditions?

If times got tough again, we could always leave, but we felt concern for our friends. We had heard that a KGB agent threatened a Christian in another town, "You are free now, but we have a file that thick on all of you. When the time is right, we'll use it." (p.187-188)

CONNECT or REFLECT:
As a child, what did you fear most?

STUDY AND DISCUSS:
Is God leading you—or is life taking you—down a path that makes you uneasy in some way? Explain.

Compare the response of the ten spies with that of Joshua and Caleb. Num. 13:17-33, 14:1-11. Record Joshua's words of faith.

Note the situation and words of encouragement.
Ex. 14:10-14

Deut. 31:1-8

Mat. 1:20-21

Our source of fear is often not a result of direct threat or intimidation. We might fear our own sense of inadequacy, fear the future, or fear that which lies beyond our control. How does fear affect you?

1 Jn. 4:18a says: "There is no fear in love. But perfect love drives out fear," How or why does love drive out fear?

Describe a time you experienced this truth.

How does this truth, "perfect love drives out fear," relate to the following verses?
Heb. 13:5-6

Rom. 8:35-39

Ps. 27:1-3

Ps. 34:4

Ps. 56:3-4

Ps. 94:14,18-19

Ps. 118:4-7

Is. 41:10

Luke 12:32

PRAYER OF APPLICATION:

QUOTE from Chapter 25 — "Blessed Inconveniences"

The featured speaker at the women's conference, Elisabeth Elliot, gave convicting and challenging messages. She became a widow as a young missionary when Auca Indians killed her husband. Even though she had been through tough times, she never encouraged self-pity. Her meaty talks helped me more than if she had said, "You poor dears, I know just how you feel."

She spoke on the value and necessity of suffering. "If Christ, our Lord, suffered, why should we expect anything different?" She defined suffering as "having what you don't want, or wanting what you don't have." Hard times help shape our character, she said, to make us more like Christ. God makes all things work together for good if we give our difficulties to Him. In acceptance, there is peace.

She talked about "blessed inconveniences." After that session, a leader asked us to tell someone nearby about something we found difficult. I thought of how people used the entryway to our apartment building as a toilet. I was used to the urine smell but we got a more solid "present" the previous week. I finally cleaned it up, since it didn't go away by wishful thinking.

"Now," the leader said, "Thank God for your area of difficulty."

Could I be truly thankful for this? I *could* be thankful that Jesus left a perfectly pure and clean realm to live in a polluted world.

In another session, Elisabeth Elliot told the story of a woman who dealt with a series of difficulties, including the sickness and death of her mother. The stress could have crushed her but with each new crisis, she continued to say, "For this, I have Jesus."

After returning home, I found another "blessed inconvenience" in the entryway. I took our garbage pail and a piece of thin cardboard down the stairs, trying to be grateful for the opportunity to serve my neighbors. *For this, I have Jesus.* (p.193)

CONNECT or REFLECT:

What is an area of difficulty, or a "blessed inconvenience," for you?

STUDY AND DISCUSS:
Read 1 Thes. 5:18. How can we be thankful in all circumstances?

1 Cor. 10:1-13. In what ways did God provide for the Israelites?

How did they respond?

Note verse 10. Also read Num. 11:1-6; 16:41-50. Why was God so hard on the complainers? What is so bad about grumbling?

Identify at least one person in the Bible who made the best of a difficult situation or series of difficulties and could "bloom where planted."

Read Gen. 37, 39, 40. List the situations that could have led to self-pity or bitterness.

Identify the people and groups of people in these chapters to whom Joseph was a blessing. Also include Gen. 41:53-57 and Gen. 45:7-11.

How does changing our question from, "Why me, God?" to "What would you have me do now, God?" help us move forward?

Read Acts. 16:16-34. What happened that could have led to self-pity or bitterness? How did Paul and Silas respond? What did God do?

How would God want you to respond in your area of difficulty? (Your response to this lesson's first question.)

PRAYER OF APPLICATION:

27 - PERSEVERANCE

QUOTE from Chapter 26 — "If You Don't Lose Heart"

"Have you thought more about whether or not we should come back to Ukraine after our furlough?" Cory asked. We had given ourselves until the end of the year to make a decision.

I hadn't forgotten. "What are you thinking?" I replied.

"Sometimes I just want to go home, but I feel like we are able to help here in ways we can't in the U.S. But I know it's hard for you here and I don't want to stay if you don't."

One year had passed since my friend Vicky said, "You can't make a decision based on whether or not something is hard." I had replayed her words many times.

Gal. 6:9 also challenged me toward perseverance: "Let us not become weary in doing good, for at the proper time we will reap a harvest if we do not give up." I didn't want to give up too soon and miss seeing the results of our labor.

While wrestling with the decision, I thought of the horses we had on the farm while I was growing up. When I broke a young filly, she would jerk on the rope, shake her head, and run in circles. I had been like that horse. Resisting takes a lot of energy. Life is easier when walking submissively, letting God take the lead.

"No, it's not an easy place to live," I told Cory, "but I am able to live here. I feel like we're supposed to come back too."

After I stopped fighting with God, life in Ukraine became more enjoyable. Sure, our water and electricity continued to go off—and the apartment entrance still smelled like an outhouse—but I stopped looking for things to justify my discontent. (p.199)

CONNECT or REFLECT:

What activity, sport, or hobby have you done that required perseverance?

STUDY AND DISCUSS:
What is the relationship between the ability to accept unpleasant
circumstances and the ability to persevere?

What is the relationship between our ability to trust God's leading and the
ability to accept or face difficult circumstances?

Note phrases from the following verses that apply to this question.
Job 2:9-10

Job 23:9-10

Duet. 32:3-4

Ps. 31:14-15

Is. 45:9-11

What was God's motive when leading the Israelites through hard times?
Deut. 8:2-16

What are the rewards of endurance?
Gal. 6:9

Ps. 126:5-6

1 Cor. 15:57-58

2 Tim 2:10

2 Tim 2:11-12

Heb. 10:35-36

Heb. 6:10-12

What is an area where you believe God would have you persevere?

How do we persevere?

How do the following verses help answer that question?
Rom 15:5

Heb. 12:1-3

I Cor. 13:4a,7b

Eph 6:10-13

PRAYER OF APPLICATION:

28 - SETTING GOALS

QUOTE from Chapter 27 — Graduation

Many of the church planters spent their free week working with their home church—since it was easier—instead of trying to start new churches.

Andre told them, "You need to keep a journal. Set ministry goals each week and analyze how you spend your time. In making plans and in your evaluation, you need to ask yourself, 'How will this help me to plant a new church?'" (p.181)

One month after graduation, the church planters gathered for a seminar and to give updates on their work. Two told how they wrote a series of tracts and distributed them at five hundred apartments in town. Some church planters held an art exhibit of Christian paintings. Some showed Christian films in homes and theaters and evangelized door-to-door. One gave away New Testaments to Moslem Tatar in their own language. (p.202)

When the church planters gathered for their monthly meeting in March, Cory asked each to talk about their goals for the future. He wanted to encourage initiative, since the leaders couldn't stand over the church planters and direct their every move.

Of the eleven, only two could state a clear plan for their work. The idea of setting goals was a hard concept for most to grasp. They had grown up in a society where people at the top set the agenda and everyone else was supposed to wait for orders.

People also need stability in order to set goals. Many Americans feel they are "masters of their own destiny," but our country has simply known peace and prosperity for a long time. Those living in countries with frequent political and economic upheaval find goal setting more difficult. (p.205-206)

CONNECT or REFLECT:
What is a goal you have for the next six months?

STUDY AND DISCUSS:
Unless one sets goals and works toward them, it is easy to be distracted.
When should we "go with the flow" and when do we "swim upstream?"

How do the following verses contribute to this discussion?
John 17:4

1 Cor. 9:24-27

James 4:13-16

Give an example or two from the Bible where people set goals—or God
gave a goal—and they worked toward it.

Look up the following examples. Note the person, the goal, any
distractions or obstacles.
Josh. 1:1-9 (Skim the book of Joshua to see some obstacles: physical
barriers, attitudes, and sins.)

Mat. 16:21-23

Acts 20:17-27

The story of Nehemiah includes many elements we can apply when it comes to setting goals and working toward them. Read Nehemiah, chapters 1 and 2. Identify scripture references that correspond to the following factors.

    -He hears of a need

    -He takes it before God

    -He takes the first steps

Nehemiah experienced some good reasons to give up. What were they? How did he respond?
Neh. 2:19-20

Neh. 4:1-6

Neh. 4:7-20

Neh. 6:1-16

Sometimes we set goals that don't work out as we hope. What can we learn from the following example?
Acts 16:6-10

Read the following verses and note principles to consider when setting goals.
Prov. 16:9

Prov. 3:5-6

Prov. 19:21

PRAYER OF APPLICATION:

29 - GROWTH IN GODLINESS

QUOTE from Chapter 28 — Growing in Grace

Rob and Arlene decided to adopt a seventeen-month old boy and considered another: a fourteen-month old boy weighing less than twelve pounds. His birth weight had been normal, but he was sick most of his first year.

They held this tiny child who was so weak he could not sit unassisted. His bright eyes met theirs. They faced a decision: adopt just one or take this second boy as well? When thinking rationally, just one seemed sufficient but that answer gave them no peace.

"We prayed about it last night," Arlene said the next morning. "We believe both of them belong to us."

Many people had told us, "I could never do what you do." I felt the same about Rob and Arlene's decision, since they would soon have five children age five and under. I felt great respect for their desire to give a hope and a future to these children, but could I do it? I don't know.

God doesn't call everyone to be missionaries; nor does He call everyone to take in orphans. God gives us the grace to do what He has called us to do—and whatever it is, we are to grow in godliness.

While doing my homework for a women's Bible study, I came across 1 Timothy 4:7: "Train yourself to be godly." Godliness doesn't come naturally. I considered how spiritual training is like physical exercise. Exercise requires diligence and self-denial, but it gives strength and stamina.

Different athletes—swimmers, football players and figure skaters— have different strengths; Christians have diverse abilities too. Whatever our gift, we have room for growth in godliness. We all must step out in obedience, deny selfish inclinations, and trust God with whatever lies down the road. (p.207-208)

CONNECT or REFLECT:

What sport, club, or activity have you participated in that required training for a successful outcome?

STUDY AND DISCUSS:
God enables us to do what He calls us to do. In what ways have you
experienced God's help, His grace, for your calling?

Note "who" and "how" they received help for their calling:
Deut. 31:7-8

Judg. 6:14-16

2 Sam. 7:8-9

Jer. 1:4-9

Acts. 1:8

Phil. 4:13

2 Tim. 4:16-18

God uses ordinary people. God is the source of success, but certain
characteristics make us more usable, better able to participate in His plan
for the world. What characteristics make us more usable to God?

In what ways can you compare physical exercise to steps one might take
for spiritual growth?

Paul uses many athletic examples. What do they show about steps you can take for growth in godliness?
Phil. 3:12-14

1 Cor. 9: 24-27

1 Tim. 4:7-8

2 Tim 2:3-5

Heb. 12:11-13

Heb. 12:1-2

Acts 20:24

If Christianity was a sport you wanted to win, where would you apply more discipline?

PRAYER OF APPLICATION:

30 - GOD'S REPAYMENT PLAN

QUOTE from Chapter 29 — Reap with Rejoicing

On our first Sunday evening back, our home church asked us to give an informal update. During the question and answer portion, one woman asked, "Do you feel there is a cost to being a missionary?" Cory thought I should answer that one.

I dove in, then tried to paddle to the surface again. Yes, there is a cost. Pressures brought stress to our family and marriage. We went without outside supports nearby. We muddled through times of wondering why we didn't see God's blessing—why we didn't feel "fulfilled" after doing what we thought God wanted us to do. Only later did we experience the truth that "those who sow in tears will reap with rejoicing." We might have given up too soon.

I learned what it means to "present your body as a living sacrifice" with the physical hardships. A women's conference I attended in Ukraine helped my perspective, with speaker Elisabeth Elliot who said that Jesus suffered, so why shouldn't we suffer too? This is the normal Christian life: to offer our lives as a sacrifice to Christ.

Afterward, I thought more about this woman's question and felt my answer was incomplete. Sure, there is a cost to being a missionary, but there is also a cost to being a parent. Every worthwhile undertaking has a price tag.

I don't want to focus on the cost so much that I forget God's repayment plan. Jesus said, "I will never leave you nor forsake you." He promised those who leave father, mother, brother, sister, houses, and lands will gain them back many times over.

We saw God's faithfulness during furlough. I often met people who said, "I pray for you every day." We were surrounded by supportive fathers, mothers, brothers, and sisters. We had many houses and lands available to us. (p.214-215)

It's a privilege to participate with God in His redemptive work in the world. Andre wrote from Ukraine, saying they were working toward the goal of a church for every village of Crimea. "The number of unreached villages is intimidating, but God wants *all* people to know Him. We know the Lord will bless us in this, since it is His will. We don't know how to reach this goal, but it doesn't frighten us any more. We go forward, like we did the past two years when we could only see to the turn in the road.

The Lord is leading us and in His time, He will show us the part that lies around the bend." (p.216)

CONNECT or REFLECT:
How have you been blessed from following Jesus?

STUDY AND DISCUSS:
It has been said, "You can't out-give God." What does His "repayment plan" include?

In what ways does God bless those who follow Him?
Ps. 66:8-12

Ps. 84:11-12

Ps. 18:30-36

Ps. 29:11

Luke 12:27-32

Phil. 4:19

2 Cor. 9:6-11

Mat. 19:29

Eph. 3:20-21

1 Thes. 2:19-20

Rom. 8:17-18

2 Tim. 2:11-12a

2 Tim. 4:7-8

In what ways are you still waiting for reward, or a sense of reward?

In what ways have you already experienced God's blessing or His faithfulness?

PRAYER OF APPLICATION:

NOTES FOR GROUP LEADERS

HOW MANY WEEKS?
Although the study is divided into 30 lessons, each lesson can take more than one week to cover in group discussion, depending on the amount of time allotted and how much you dig in and discuss the questions and scriptures.

You can take the "tour bus" approach and give a quick overview. A slower-paced "walking tour" will need more time to consider and discuss how these concepts and scriptures apply to real life.

CONNECTION QUESTIONS:
Each lesson begins with a connection question, to help group members get to know each other. These simple questions provide a way to hear something from each one in the group, whether or not they participate in the rest of the discussion. Until group members know each other—or if you get new people joining – ask each person to say their name before answering the question. Encourage short answers, especially in large groups.

If you take more than one week to cover each lesson, here are ideas for more connection questions:
- What are you thankful for or how would you like prayer?
- What was your first paying job?
- What do you like to do for fun?
- What was an unexpected joy this week or month?
- As a child, what chore did you have, like or dislike?
- If you had to eat the same thing for breakfast every day, what would it be?
- What is one of the riskiest things you remember doing?
- What was the greatest challenge you faced in the past year? Where did you find your resources to meet that challenge?
- If you could recapture one quality you had as a child, what would it be?
- What aspect of life on earth would you like to have in heaven?
- What is your favorite fruit?
- What was your favorite pet growing up?
- What is the worst storm you remember?
- If you were in trouble late at night and needed help, who would you call?
- What is your favorite meal?
- What food did you dislike growing up?
- New Years: What would you like to see happen this year?
- What is your favorite thing about Spring (Summer, Fall, Winter)?
- Thanksgiving: Where did you usually have Thanksgiving dinner, as a child?
- Christmas: What was a memorable gift?

STUDY AND DISCUSS – ASK QUESTIONS!

I hope this Bible study guide will engage the heart and mind of those who use it. The leader doesn't need to have all the answers, just the ability to ask questions. Go beyond accepting the obvious "fill in the blank" answers. Ask questions to help participants dig deeper. If someone asks a question, don't feel you need to provide the answer, but ask, "How would the rest of you answer that?" (This promotes discussion, brings out ideas you may not have, and gives you more time to think.) Here are other ideas for promoting discussion.

- What stands out to you in this passage?
- What else?
- What does it mean to…..? (ie "to pick up your cross daily")
- What do you notice about this scripture?
- Tell me more about that. (If you want explanation of a short answer.)
- How does that apply to us?
- What gems can we pull out of these verses?
- What encouragement do you find here?
- Good, what else?
- If you were to explain this to someone who had never heard it before, what would you say?
- What questions come to mind as you read this?
- How would the rest of you answer that?
- What cross-references do you have, for other scriptures, that might give more clarity? Any footnotes?
- What does that look like in real life?
- Who is someone who implements this?
- How has this worked in your life?
- How about the rest of you?
- Someone else?

Some "bunny trails" can be useful, but keep the main goal in mind: to gain "strength for the journey." Return focus to the lesson, if needed. If the discussion shows someone needs prayer, take time out to pray.

PRAYER OF APPLICATION:

Set aside a time for prayer at the end, encouraging group members to reflect on highlights of the lesson.

- What was useful? What do you need to do?
- Respond to God either silently or out-loud.
- "Thank you that…" Or "Help me to…."

A designated person can give the final closing prayer.

Books
to encourage and challenge

by Janice Lemke

Five Loaves and
Two Bowls of Borscht

Finding Strength
for the Journey

Steppes of Faith

info@purposepress.net

www.purposepress.net

NOTES OR PRAYER REQUESTS

CPSIA information can be obtained
at www.ICGtesting.com
Printed in the USA
BVHW042138210619
551637BV00008B/490/P

9 780984 594917